Notebook

Notebook

date:

Notebook

date:

Notebook

Notebook

date:

Notebook   date:

Notebook

date:

Notebook

date:

Notebook

date:

Notebook

Notebook

date:

Notebook

Notebook

date:

Notebook

date:

Notebook

date:

Notebook

date:

Notebook

Notebook

Notebook

date:

Notebook

date:

Notebook

date:

Notebook

date:

Notebook

date:

Notebook

date:

Notebook

date:

Notebook   date:

Notebook

date:

Notebook

date:

Notebook

date:

Notebook

date:

Notebook

Notebook

date:

Notebook

date:

Notebook

Notebook

date:

Notebook

Notebook

date:

Notebook

date:

Notebook

date:

Notebook

date:

Notebook

date:

Notebook

date:

Notebook

date:

Notebook

date:

Notebook

date:

Notebook

date:

Notebook

date:

Notebook

Notebook

date:

Notebook

Notebook

date:

Notebook

date:

Notebook

Notebook

date:

Notebook

Notebook

Notebook

date:

Notebook

Notebook

date:

Notebook

Notebook

Notebook

Notebook

date:

Notebook

Notebook

date:

Notebook

date:

Notebook

Notebook

date:

Notebook

date:

Notebook

date:

Notebook

date:

Notebook

date:

Notebook

date:

Notebook

date:

Notebook

date:

Notebook

date:

Notebook

date:

Notebook

date:

Notebook

date:

Notebook

date:

Notebook

date:

Notebook

date:

Notebook

Notebook

date:

Notebook

date:

Notebook   date:

Notebook

date:

Notebook

date:

Notebook

date:

Notebook

date:

Notebook

date:

Notebook

date:

Notebook

date:

Notebook

date:

Notebook

date:

Notebook

Notebook

date:

Notebook

date:

Notebook

date:

Notebook

Notebook

date:

Notebook

Notebook

date:

Notebook

date:

Notebook

date:

Notebook

date:

Notebook

date:

Notebook

date:

Notebook

date:

Notebook

date:

Notebook

date:

Notebook

date:

Notebook

Notebook

date:

Notebook

date:

Notebook

date:

Notebook

date:

Notebook

date:

Notebook

date:

Notebook

date:

Notebook

date:

Notebook

date:

Notebook

date:

Notebook

date:

Notebook

date:

Notebook

Notebook

date:

Notebook

date:

Notebook

date:

Notebook

Notebook

date:

Notebook

date:

Notebook

date:

Notebook

Notebook

date:

Notebook

Notebook

date:

Notebook   date:

Notebook

date:

Notebook

date:

Notebook

date:

Notebook

date:

Notebook

date:

Notebook

Notebook

date:

Notebook

date:

Notebook

date:

Notebook

Notebook

date:

Notebook

date: